Belly of the Beast

Version 3.0 – Edited and updated on- Wednesday, September 22, 2021

Written by
Denny Magic

This book is appropriate for all readers.

Table of Contents

Dedication

This book is dedicated to my wife Nancy Alford, who passed away on Wednesday, December 28th, 2016, at five-thirty in the morning. I had just completed the first draft of this book, and I was anxious to show it to her later that day. She never had a chance to read it.

She was my partner, my friend, my editor, and my enabler. She allowed me to be creative, and she did everything that she possibly could so that I could shine.

Backstory

My first task is to tell you a little bit about myself, and how I ended up working for the General Motors Assembly Plant in Fremont, California.

My journey, which ultimately led me to General Motors, began while I was visiting a friend of mine (Hank Clark) at the Clark's home in Fremont. While I was waiting for Hank to get ready, I stepped out into their garage where Hank's younger brother Jim was engaged in a budding home business of building custom Harley-Davidson Motorcycles.

> Jim was a talented fellow, and extremely business savvy. In later life, he founded the successful **James Gasket Company** in Dayton, Nevada. He was so successful (internationally) that his name (and his company) ended up in the Motorcycle Hall of Fame.

But that day, in the Clark's garage... Jim showed me a custom painted frame, tank and rear fender that was designed by a very talented artist from Hayward, CA... by the name of Harry Browne.

Jim was familiar with me and my artistic capabilities, as I had hung around with his older brother for several years by that time. I was a neighbor, who lived just a block away. In addition, Jim and I attended the same high school, so he had an opportunity to observe my involvement with the arts.

He was also intuitive enough to know that as an artist, I might turn out to be a valuable resource for his business. By showing me this custom artwork from Harry Browne, Jim probably thought that he'd be able to hedge his bet in case Mr. Browne's painting services were no longer available?   If I could produce the same level of artwork that Harry Browne was capable of, the custom painting part of his motorcycle business would be uninterrupted.

If so, he'd have a second artist who could pick up the slack when his budding business took off.

The bottom-line was that I knew that I could certainly recreate the type of custom painting that Mr. Browne had on display in the Clark's garage that day. The only person that needed convincing was Jim.

As time went on Jim rented a Butler Building in a warehouse area right off Warm Springs Blvd. (just behind the Spin-A-Yarn restaurant), soon after I rented the space next-door to Jim's, and there I opened Uncle Sam's Custom Painting.

By that time Jim was convinced that I could paint anything, and he often hired me to do just that, as his business prospered.

Jim's company evolved from building custom motorcycles, to putting together gasket kits for Harley-Davidson motors, and over the years that part of his business grew so huge that he eventually became the sole supplier of gaskets to The Harley-Davidson Company.

We were next door neighbors for about eight years, and both companies seemed to complement each other.

During that time, I did indeed paint custom motorcycles... However, I also painted custom artwork on vans and cars for auto-dealerships, and individual customers alike... I also painted boats, dragsters, and I even painted several sets of conga drums and guitars for another company that had a shop across from Jim and I, called King-Konga®.

While the popularity of custom paint on vehicles expanded Uncle Sam's business... We also entered (and frequently won awards) at several California Custom Car & Motorcycle shows, up and down the state of California.

Many of our bikes and vehicles were featured in Custom Motorcycle and Car Magazines, which always helped my company attract new customers.

Ironically, even though we were competitors... I painted Plexiglas-Show-Signs and some bikes for Arlen Ness, who usually hired Harry Browne to do his painting.

In fact, one of Arlen's bikes, which Uncle Sam's painted, ended up on display, as a featured motorcycle at the Oakland California - Museum of Fine Arts.

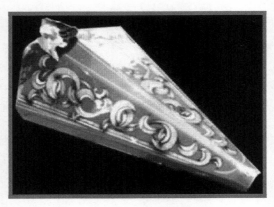

During this time, my first wife came onboard as an artist, and she was responsible for doing a lot of hand painting for Uncle Sam's like the sample below. Her style was different than my own, and this helped us appeal to customers with differing taste.

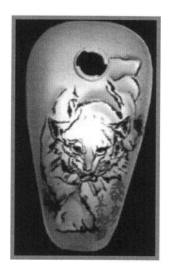

There was nothing that we couldn't, or wouldn't paint when asked, and the subject matter ran the gambit from cartoon characters to realistic depictions of authentic animals.

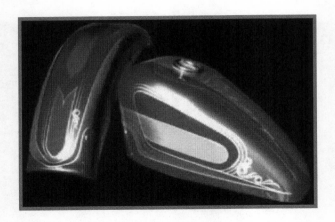

Eventually after nearly a decade, the first recession set in, and soon my customers were more interested in buying refrigerators, and washers instead of spending their money on fixing up their motorcycles, boats, and vans.

Thankfully, I had invested time and money to construct a small one-bedroom efficiency on the second floor of the building that my business was located in. The idea was that when I had to pull an 'all-nighter', I had a place to stay where I could nap, fix a meal, and shower before heading home.

When the business all but dried up, my wife expressed the idea that maybe we could move into the shop until things picked up. So, my first wife; with her two kids in tow, me, our wonderful dog Damon, along with an outstanding cat named Smokey all moved into the warehouse, hoping for better times. I suspect that we were one of the first inhabitants of what is today, a 'tiny-house' craze.

As the months dragged on, things did not improve, and finally my wife heard about an opening at the Ford Plant in Milpitas. The good news was that she got the job, and suddenly we could pay our bills again.

As my custom painting business dropped off, it finally ceased to exist. That's when I wondered if I could get a job with Ford, like my wife? I reasoned that with two of us making the same great wages, which people in the automotive business were earning... That we'd be financially set.

The first reality-check was that I was unable to acquire gainful employment at the Ford Plant. That was not going to happen.

Then... As things started to change at home, my wife left Ford, and went to work at General Motors. The good news was it was even closer to our little make-shift apartment.

General motors was just on the other side of the railroad tracks that separated us from the plant. If you had a good pitching arm, you could have easily thrown a rock into the back-parking-lot of General Motors from our building.

There is no doubt that my wife was a hard worker. Unfortunately, she also had a propensity to 'play hard', and while working at GM she began an affair with a co-worker which ended our marriage.

Soon after, I found myself living alone with my Cat and Dog in that drafty warehouse.

That's when I decided that I could try getting work at GM, and if I could attain that goal... the money would come in very handy. I even reasoned that if I could get on their night shift... then I could sleep in my warehouse apartment during the day, when it was warmer. That way I could work all night when it was too damned cold in there - to sleep comfortably.

MY company's assets and tax refund were divided in half because of the divorce, and with the money I was left with, I decided to invest in myself, so I could get a job for myself at GM.

I put it that way, because I had already been dropping off an application with the gate guard every week or two, for a couple of months, to no avail.

That's when I took a blank GM Application to my printer, the same fellow that I had used for all my custom painting business's, printing needs. I filled out the GM application on both sides with a red ink pen, by using two sheets of tracing paper.

Then the printer printed 100 copies of the GM Application in black ink first... so they were unmistakably from the originals... and then he used the tracing paper to print my personal information in Red ink, which made it look like I had filled out every application by hand.

The next day I dropped one off in the morning with the day shift guard, and then a second copy that night, with the night shift guard. I did this every day for a about a month. That's when GM's personnel department finally had enough, and I was called in for an interview.

The first thing that the personnel director said to the gathering job seekers was "Is Denny here? Please raise your hand?"

I raised my hand and he said... "Now... Will you please stop with the applications?"

After everyone laughed, he explained that GM had a huge stack of my applications, and they hoped that by hiring me, I'd stop dropping applications off at the front gate? But he did congratulate me for being so inventive. He added that no one before, had ever tried that technique.

That is how I ended up getting hired at General Motors.

After the orientation process was completed, a very nice fellow arrived to escort me to my work station. He was not the typical stogy old fart executive, and I found him to be very personable, even if he was wearing a tie which announced that he was part of the GM hierarchy.

When we arrived in the "Truck - Frame Department" he explained that my job was... As the frames came down the assembly line, hanging upside down by chain, I was to read the manifest to figure out which leaf springs would have to be installed on my side, of that specific truck frame.

Initially it seemed like a relatively easy task, seeing as there was only one front leaf spring, and one back leaf spring. That is, until I realized that leaf springs weighed from 75 to 115 lbs. each. Keep in mind... the assembly line never stopped moving, so you had to be quick and efficient.

As I emptied steel boxes full of leaf springs, some bastard (driving a fork lift) brought me a fresh box of springs every few minutes. He was very efficient, and thus I never ran out of leaf springs. That became my personal nightmare.

The nicest thing that he did for me, was to keep the heaviest springs at the closest possible position. But his thoughtfulness was not as valuable as it seemed, seeing as even the 75 lb. springs could be 20 – 40 feet away from the actual installation site. And remember... the line was automated and never stopped moving.

I had to lift each spring from a 6' x 6' by 3' tall steel box and walk it over to the moving frame, then hoist it up, until it dropped into small steel cups that were welded onto each truck frame. I also had an over-sized fanny pack around my waste which contained 40 – 50 steel mounting bolts.

All I had to do was hoist the correct front spring up to waste height and set it into the mounting cups, then slide in a bolt at each end. Then I'd go and retrieve the back spring and repeat the process onto the rear section of the frame. The next person on the line tightened those bolts, and every few minutes I had to replenish my bag of bolts!

However, within the first thirty minutes, I was an expert spring installer. But by lunch I was starting to get damned sore.

When I returned from lunch another fellow came up to talk with me.

The unnerving thing about his visit was that he was in two arm casts, and he introduced himself as the "Former Leaf Spring Installer". Apparently, he was the fellow that I was hired to replace.

He explained that he was 'out on disability' because this job had landed him in the hospital. I asked him how long he had worked the job before being injured, and he said just a little more than a week.

After this guy left the area, I immediately called the foreman over and told him that I wanted to meet with the "suit". The guy who originally brought me down to this work station.

I didn't see that fellow until the end of the second day. By that time, my arms looked exactly like Popeye's! The muscles were all distended and my lower arms were swelled up so huge, that they resembled the thickness of my thighs.

I knew that I would end up in arm casts before the week was up if I didn't quit, and I had already decided that I was done with GM. If the guy in the tie didn't show up today, I would not be there a third day.

The nice fellow (in the tie) finally showed up, and he got the foreman to get a relief worker to take my job over, so we could talk

As we were walking down the aisle, I told him that this was my last day. He was shocked and did his best to talk me out of that, and when he saw my arms, and realized that my mind was already made up... he asked, **"Well, let me ask... what did you do before you came here?"**

I noticed that he was holding a rolled up Custom Van Magazine, in his hand.

So, I pointed at his magazine and I said, **"That's what I used to do!"**

He stopped walking, and unfurled the magazine and asked, **"What"** and I pointed at the cover while saying, **"I used to do custom painting on Vans, Boats, Cars, Dragsters and Custom Motorcycles."**

He nodded his head, and then held up a single digit and said, **"OK. Go back to what you were doing, and I'll be back within a half hour. I promise! I think I have a much better job for a guy with your skills."**

Within a few minutes, true to his word, he came back. He had the foreman get the relief guy to come over to do my job, and this executive and I took a long walk over to a new department at the opposite end of the plant, that was called "'Paint Repair'". I say 'long-walk' because that assembly plant was nearly a mile long from end to end.

Now this guy was 100% straight with me, and on that walk he explained that because the department that he was taking me to, was considered a 'Prime Assignment', everyone who worked at GM wasn't picked to work there. He intimated that it was considered a privilege to be selected.

At first I wasn't too trusting, but as it turned out, he was totally correct in his analysis.

Because this new assignment was considered 'a privilege', GM expected all the "Paint Repair'" workers to put in much longer hours than the line-workers. That was the 'trade off' for getting a position with "Paint Repair".

He explained that when the assembly line stopped after nine hours and everyone else went home, the "'Paint Repair'" department was expected to remain on the job for an addition four hours each day. That meant that my days would be around 14 hours when you added in lunch.

Then he added, "Paint Repair is also expected to work every other weekend. Meaning that I would only have four days per month - off."

The good news was that anything over eight hours per day was paid at time and a half. Saturday and Sundays were calculated at double time, and if there was a holiday that fell on any work day, that I would be paid triple time.

He also added that because we were like GM's last resort to find and fix flaws... That's why we were treated almost like emergency room doctors who were on-call to attend to any problem that came up.

This meant that there was very little work for this department to do on most shifts, unlike regular workers who were on-the-assembly-line who had to keep pace with the moving conveyor belt.

Our job was based on a hit-and-miss principal, meaning that something had to be wrong with a specific truck's paint job before our department every saw it.

It was up to a special inspector (Jim Haggard) that marked trucks with a problem. Jim would then drive that vehicle off the line, and park it in a special area outside. Then after the main line went down for the night, and all the regular workers went home, Jim would start retrieving the earmarked trucks and drive them back inside to our area where we would fix them.

After pondering my situation, I surmised that because I was still young enough (and now a single man again) that the prospects of earning all that money, with hardly any time to spend any of it... seemed like a great idea. Subsequently, I accepted my new position in "Paint Repair" and that is where my story begins...

Paint Repair – Day One

Just like any new job, I was greeted by all the various members of the 'Paint Repair' crew. It was quite a mix of characters, and each had a unique story attached to them.

Because I waited so many years before writing this story, I am confident that when I mention someone by name... It is likely that those folks are no longer with us. And for those that still are, I hope that they understand that unless I specifically point out that person's flaws... I hold everyone who worked there in the highest regard.

Teddy (can't remember his last name) was the one and only body-man in the 'Paint Repair' Department. His skill was to fill dents and scratches with lead, which was certainly a lost art by the time.

He almost always worked alone at the very head of the 'Paint Repair' area. If a truck did not have a dent or a scratch, he wasn't required to do anything. He was the only area in this department that had a radio.

Then there was Emmitt Workman, Paul Chin, Tony Contreras, Dean Gillespie, Emile, Juan, and Ralph, who were the main maskers, tapers, and sanders. Again, if I can't recall some of their last names, then it will not appear in this book.

Then there was Don Pardini, and Steve Workman (Emmitt's son) who were our spray painters.

Each side of the 'Paint Repair' department had several pneumatic sanders that were passed back and forth on the main work floor. And each man had an air blower tool, and a belt hook that held a roll of masking tape.

Each sanding man waited for one of the taping guys to finish masking off the damaged area, then they'd hit the problem area with the sander, and blow off the dust with a blower, before sending that specific truck on its way into the spray booth.

That's when one of us would drive the prepared truck into the spray booth, setting the front wheels onto the automated track which pulled the rest of the truck completely into the spray booth.

Once inside, Don or Steve would select the right colored feeder hose, and they would spray the damaged area with the appropriate color, then the truck would automatically move down the track, into a short oven section, where the paint was cooked for approximately twenty-minutes until it was dry to the touch, and when it came out the other end... there was Emmett Workman and his girlfriend who would peel off the tape. I am sorry; but I cannot remember the name of Emmitt's girlfriend?

Then Emmett would drive the truck about fifty feet over to another area called the 'Short-Line' where it would pass over a pit that had a half dozen mechanics waiting down below to fix anything mechanical.

If there was nothing wrong (mechanically) with the vehicle, then the mechanics in the pit would ignored it. Then, as it moved down the 'Short-Line' until it reached the end... a driver was waiting there to take it outside, where it was parked in a 'good-to-go' area.

The drivers took turns driving the finished trucks either outside to park them, or when the work tag indicated that the problem still existed... they drove those trucks back around and placed them back on the 'Short-Line' for another pass. Sometimes a truck would cycle several times until it was finally fixed.

Being a driver; off the 'Short-Line', was considered one of the best jobs in the plant. Drivers came to work in decent street clothes, and never had to wear overalls. The mood there was totally casual. Usually the drivers would talk, or play cards, or read magazines waiting their turn to drive the next vehicle. Plus... All the trucks were brand new, and clean inside, which made this job very user-friendly.

In very rare cases, Emmet would take a truck and bypass the 'Short-Line' altogether, bringing it back around to 'Paint Repair' if a blemish or a scratch wasn't repaired correctly. Or... IF our crew missed something off the main work order.

The 'Paint Repair' Department had its own foreman, when I first arrived... most of the foremen in 'Paint Repair' had very little to do, and they changed frequently.

Because the guys working in 'Paint Repair' didn't need supervision. I would guess that working down there as a foreman was probably considered boring by most if not all of them.

The foreman that was there when I arrived for my first day, hardly said two words to me. In fact, he seemed a little bit cranky, he told me which one, of the two rows, that I would be working at, and he walked away. Mr. Personality he wasn't!

Thankfully the 'pain-in-the-ass' foreman that we had, seemed to change fairly frequently and the assholes didn't stay long... One or two of them had huge egos, and what I refer to as Hitler complexes. But surprisingly, many of them turned out to be great bosses!

As the days moved forward I realized that the men who worked there, sort of managed themselves. When our shift started, we would just try to equally divide in half at the start of each day... depending on who did what, or... who didn't, show up for work. Many choices were made because men formed bonds with other men and choose coworkers that they enjoyed working with.

One half of us would assemble on one side, feeding trucks into one spray booth, and the rest of us gravitated towards the other side.

One of the more experienced guys (Emmett) whose job it was to pull the paper and tape at the end of the drying ovens seemed to know more about the department than the various foreman did, and soon I realized that being a foreman in the 'Paint Repair' Department may have been like being exiled to Siberia. However, for all intent and purposes, Emmett seemed to run the show, and even some of these temporary foremen learned to rely on Emmitt.

It seemed, that the higher ups, may have stuck a foreman who maybe wasn't well liked upstairs... down in 'Paint Repair' to get rid of him. This was speculation on my part, and I did not know this to be a fact, for sure?

The bottom-line was... workers in 'Paint Repair' all seemed to have specialized knowledge, even though I never did know each man's personal backstory. It just seemed that everyone knew what they were doing. So, even a top foreman had very little to do in 'Paint Repair'.

Assembly Line Commerce

After my first week in 'Paint Repair', the first thing that I learned about were the unique personalities of each man, and how many guys ran their own little businesses within the GM plant.

The immense size of the factory made it feel like you were in a small city. The plant was truly a mile long from one end to the other, and I would guess as much as a quarter mile wide.

Every type of person including former criminals, and misfits had wormed their way into General Motors. Commerce (of every kind) and 'deal making' showed up in every corner of this huge complex. This included merchandise of all kinds, food from every ethnicity, drugs, gambling, and yes... even sex.

In the 'Paint Repair' department, Juan's wife made burritos every night that he brought inside a cooler every day. He sold them for $1.50 each. Paul Chin brought in a five-gallon cooler filled with homemade lemonade every day that he made the night before and sold by the glass.

As you walked around the side of our ovens, headed towards Emmitt and his main squeeze, another guy working on the car side of the area adjacent to the truck side, had Hot Links for sale.

He had made good use of a 220-volt outlet by purchasing the necessary converters from an electrical supply house, that allowed him to convert the 220vt power to 110-volt house current.   That he used to power up his hot dog cooker/roller, which cooked his hot links, and kept them warm.

He had a TV tray setup with relish, onions, ketchup, mustard, and the buns.

Everything in the plant that was for sale was usually un-supervised. And most products (especially food items) were sold on the honor-system. If you didn't pay for something, God help you! Subsequently, no one stiffed anyone.

GM had a decent cafeteria but it was quite a walk from the 'Paint Repair' department, this meant that a good twenty minutes of your lunch might be eaten up just getting to and from the cafeteria. Plus... we all knew that if you went there, you might run into some 'wig' in a tie, who might grill you will stupidly questions about how things are going.

An egocentric big shot, always wanted to question employees about productivity or some such nonsense, because all of them were more concerned about how big their annual bonuses were going to be at the end of the year? Back in those days, an annual bonus could amount to ten grand or more.

That Unforgettable Prick

Yet at least one of the pain-in-the-ass, 'wigs' (as we liked to call them) was unfortunately a frequent visitor to 'Paint Repair'.

The worst of them was John Engelhard who was a supervisor from the 2nd floor paint department. If you looked up "real pain in the ass" in Webster's Dictionary... You'd see John's picture! He was, simply put... a fucking prick!

John treated every young guy in the 'Paint Repair' department poorly, and he threw his weight around with a lot of unnecessary sarcasm and condescending wise-cracks that were always mean-spirited.

He always seemed to be attempting to intimidate the younger, less experienced, guys with threats that if they didn't shape up (and soon) that he'd have them transferred upstairs to the regular paint department, where they'd have to actually "Learn what real work was all about". Most of us tolerated visits by Engelhard, but behind his back we all hated him! Why?

As an example: Engelhard would sneak up behind you, and then as an example, he'd physically snatch a roll of masking tape right out of your hand and start teaching you 'how to mask'. He'd complain that you were lazy, and not moving fast enough, and thus, he'd have to show you how to tape again. He may have pulled this on you once or twice before but he was so damned ignorant, that he must have forgotten his last lesson. Truth be told, I am convinced that he enjoyed intimidating all of us young fellows.

When this happened, many of the older and wiser guys assembled just behind this theatrical show, and they would all be a smiling audience when he was done. Not because you were getting your ass chewed out, but because Engelhard had such a theatrical delivery that he was humorous and VERY entertaining! When Engelhard turned to discover that he had drawn an audience, he'd give them a nasty look, and chastise them for standing around. Then he'd say… "OK. Now. Get back to work!"

If a so-called racist was trying to find a legitimate reason to explain why they became a racist, all they would have to do is bring up the name John Engelhard.

Gentleman Emile

Speaking of African Americans... One of the nicest fellows that I worked with was Emile. I thought of this fine gentleman many times over the years, and he certainly deserved my respect as much then, as he does today.

In fact, once I was introduced to Morgan Freeman in later life, I realized how much Mr. Freeman reminded me of Emile.

Emile was a very soft-spoken fellow who had a wonderful sense of humor. He did not volunteer too much when it came to conversation, or story telling... But he was one hell of a listener, and when he did say something it was profound.

Emile always drove a brand-new Lincoln Continental. I don't know if he bought a new one every year, but that car [and him] were synonymous. Even dressed up in his crusty overalls for work, you could tell that Emile was clearly a class act.

Paul the Gambler

Paul Chin was despite what he might have thought about himself... was a very humorous man. I don't think he ever actually cracked a smile the whole time I worked with him, but he was (in my humble opinion) very funny.

Sometimes you had to look at him a second time, to make sure he was not serious. Often he espoused words of wisdom in a very comical way, that had all of us cracking up.

Paul was the fellow that brewed home-made lemonade every night in a huge upright cooler. He'd haul that thing in; and set it on a workbench that ran parallel to where we worked on the incoming trucks. Then he'd set out a bunch of large plastic cups, and a little bowl to collect a buck from everyone who wanted to sample his lemonade. He managed to sell out every day.

Over at the little break area, were four picnic style tables and benches stood, every day at lunch (and after work) a fellow from the 'Short-Line" area by the name of Joe brought in a boxed-set of professional clay gambling chips, and he would exchange them for cash with several of the regular gamblers, and all through lunch (and after work) the same eight or ten guys would play various forms of poker... Paul and Emile were regulars.

On a side note: On several occasions, I spotted gambling pots that were well over $3,000.00 on a single game, so you can imagine how serious this activity was to these men?

Juan the Burrito-guy

Juan didn't do too well with English, so there was a lot of sign language whenever you tried to converse with him. He was (at heart) a kind soul, but he had a very short fuse.

Often he'd misunderstood what you were trying to say, and he often thought that you were attempting to be rude or something, so you had to be careful about how you approached him, making sure to express your intentions so he could understand you properly.

Juan was the fellow whose wife made chicken and beef burritos every night, and he brought them in a huge Igloo® cooler. He sold his burritos for $1.50 each and for $3 - $5 you could have a decent meal. They weren't too large but they were unmistakably homemade and sumptuous.

Emmitt the Sudo-Foreman

Emmitt was a very decent guy who listened to you carefully, and always seemed to have a good answer. He never acted pious, or better than anyone else, and mostly he kept to himself at the other end of the oven where he obviously enjoyed fraternizing with his girlfriend. In fact, we rarely saw his girlfriend, and truthfully I can't even remember her name. She rarely visited us at the opposite end of the ovens.

After I was working in 'Paint Repair' for a short time, Emmitt's son Steve Workman was discharged out of the service and Emmitt helped him secure a job in 'Paint Repair' as a spray painter.

He shared that position with our other spray painter – Don Pardini. Steve and Don were not conversationalists, and mostly kept to themselves inside the actual spray booths.

Teddy, the Body-Man

Teddy was a very pleasant Japanese man who I'd have to guess was in his early fifties when I first met him. I mentioned earlier that he was a wizard with metal and was still (at that time) using lead to fill dents and scratches in vehicles that suffered some sort of damage.

I used to walk over to his little cubby-hole and spend time watching him finesse a dent right out of existence. What an artist! One day he asked me if I fish.

I explained that I "Have" been fishing but did not consider myself a fisherman. That's when he surprised me by inviting me to go fishing with him on our very rare days off.

Together we went deep-sea-fishing out of Pillar Point in Half Moon Bay, and we even departed from the Fisherman's Wharf in San Francisco on one trip. I enjoyed Teddy's company; he was a pleasure to be with.

Dean, the Pretty-Boy

Dean Gillespie was a guy in his mid-thirties. Every day when he arrived for work, he was dressed impeccably! His hair was always razor-cut and perfect like a 'Ken Doll', with not a single hair out of place.

He walked into work daily with his girlfriend who worked elsewhere in the plant, and he went to the locker room area between the two spray booths where he'd change into a pair of brand new overalls that we all swear he must have washed and pressed at home in preparation for work.

Poor Dean was the brunt of a lot of ridicule from all the guys behind his back, as he was ALWAYS looking like he was about to attend some high-class party, and not going to GM to work.

Later I would learn that Dean's father was a big shot with Harrah's Casino at Lake Tahoe, CA.

This I would discover one day; when he brought in a half dozen leisure suits on hangers, that he explained came from his father. I purchased one for $30.00, which I don't believe that I ever actually put on. But the bottom line was that Dean was the kind of the guy [from high school] that everyone might have referred to as a nerd.

Deep down inside I always like Dean and felt a little bit sorry for how the other guys seemed to treat him. I would consider myself about half-guilty when it came to Dean.

Once he told me where he had his hair cut in the Irvington District of Fremont, I visited his barbers. And when I mentioned that I worked with Dean, both barbers looked at one another and then laughed. Then they said, "You work with that nut?" ridiculing him.

Then they added that he came in two to three times a week to have his hair razor-cut and coffered. They added that neither one of them could understand it, as he always dropped around $30.00 every time they saw him, and he was a big tipper. That's when I finally understood how important appearance was to Dean.

Ralph, the Cuban

Ralph was an interesting character with a great sense of humor. I would typecast him as a "Cuban-Philosopher" as he always had something to say that was somewhat profound.

His practical-joker side was rampant. 'Paint Repair' was in an area where a lot of people from other parts of the plant came strolling by frequently on their way to one place or another. And when that happened... Ralph would often come over and stand close-by. Then he'd lean over and say, "Watch this."

Now you need to understand that any automobile assembly plant is a noisy environment. There's machinery running everywhere. Some is stopping, and some is starting up, so sound is difficult at best to isolate from where it's coming from.

Once Ralph had set his sights on you as his next target... he would either whistle loudly, or yell "Hey!" at the unsuspecting person, and then he'd immediately duck, or act like he was working on the truck in front of him.

The person would stop and start looking all around, and this would send Ralph into hysterics, and he'd have to hide behind the truck body as he bent over laughing uncontrollably.

All the guys witnessing this, started laughing too, but I suspect that they were mostly laughing at Ralph's reaction, and not the person who he was teasing.

However, there was one Czechoslovakian fellow who came down almost every night to drive trucks off the 'Short-Line", and every night... Ralph got him.

The guy finally figured out that someone was screwing with him, but over the years he never figured out who it was. Sad to say, he was a great source of laughter for the rest of us, and I admit that I'm a little bit ashamed that I participated in this Tom Foolery.

Tony, the Squirt

Tony Contreras was the youngest guy to work in 'Paint Repair'. He was probably about twenty-two when he worked with me. I liked Tony quite a bit, he was fun to be around, most of the time... but he had very little respect for anyone in authority that tried to push him around.

I would not classify him as a troublemaker or anything as serious as that, but he was very young and somewhat mischievous, and always looking for some way to dodge his responsibilities, if he could.

The best foreman that we ever had (Larry Pimentel) had Tony figured out right from the start and he knew how to handle him.

Tony seemed to like me, and he allowed me to rib him from time to time knowing full well that I meant him no harm, and he was never offended in any way, but instead just laughed at my jokes. For example, during our affiliation I gave him the nick-name of K.O.F.O.

So instead of calling him Tony, I called him KOFO.

When he finally became so curious about what that might mean, he asked me. I told him that it stood for... King of Fuck Offs.

This cracked him up, and years after GM was but a memory, Tony and I hung out together and even had some business involvement with regards to the music business. I never heard from him after that, but I always wished him the very best!

Jim, the Work-Maker

Jim Haggard worked on the main line while it was up and running during the first part of the day, until most of the plant workers went home around 2 AM.

During that time, it was his job to inspect each truck, looking for real damage (dents and scratches) and sometimes 'creating damage' when he could see that our department might have nothing to fix after the main line went home.

When he found (or created) a problem, he'd stay with that truck until it came off the main line, then he'd drive it outside and park it in a special area that was set aside as 'potential-jobs' for 'Paint Repair' to work on later. Once that vehicle was parked he'd walk back into the plant and resume his inspection tasks.

We never saw Jim in our area until after the main line went home, and then only when he was bringing all those trucks back inside for us to fix.

It was a love hate relationship, as seeing Jim meant that there was something else to fix. But realistically we all knew that Jim was probably the reason that we all still had jobs. This was my first lesson in how to keep up appearances.

When the trucks were coming off the main line in almost perfect condition, later that morning we'd suddenly get a slew of scratched glove box doors, or scratched ashtrays. That's when we knew that Jim was only trying to help us justify the expense of keeping the 'Paint Repair" department busy.

Jim knew that it was easy for us to pull a glove box door off a truck, run a sander over it for one or two seconds, lay it on a piece of paper that was taped down to the hood, and send it into the spray booth. An ash tray was equally easy to prepare. Both could be prepped in under a minute.

However, if a 'wig' came around to spy on us, our area could be full of trucks, and activity, and they'd have no complaints.

Jim had purchased that little motel at the top of the hill as you come into Jackson, CA... and that was why he was working at GM.

Larry, the Foreman

During my time in 'Paint Repair' without a doubt the BEST foreman that we ever had was Larry Pimentel.

Larry was probably in his early sixties, and I suspect that they sent him down to work in 'Paint Repair' because he was approaching retirement... It certainly wasn't to punish him in any way. I would suspect that this was done so he could take it easy for a while before he retired from GM.

Larry almost immediately took me under his wing, and started mentoring me, and his advice was dead-on, so I listened carefully. Larry had suffered through a 'bout with throat cancer, and although he almost lost his voice... he survived.

In all my time in "Paint Repair' working under him, he never steered me wrong.

As we became acquainted, I discovered that his son ran a successful travel agency in San Jose, and that every year he could vacation in some far-off country.

One year; he told me that he would be "Going to Germany this year." And I casually said that I always admired those big beer steins that they make over there.

Much to my surprise... When Larry returned from that vacation he handed me a paper sack and said immediately... "Put this in your locker and open it at home."

When I arrived at my home later that morning, I opened it to discover an elaborate German Beer Stein with a sterling silver lid. I was not only thrilled, but quite touched with his over-the-top kindness.

After that, Larry took on a kind of avuncular status with me, almost like he was a grandfather that I never had.

Overall, Larry was a great foreman. When the guys put in any kind of reasonable effort, he was pleased. He had a semi-tough-guy outward appearance, but inside he was a gentleman. His raspy voice seemed to help project his tough guy persona, but once you realized that the voice was an artifact of his fight with cancer... you could see that he was a sensitive soul.

I often think about Larry and wonder what ever happened to him?

Getting Supplies with Don

One day Emmitt seemed to have something on his mind, and he came over to asked me if I wanted to go upstairs to load up a cart with our department's supplies and get them safely back to our area? This included rolls of masking paper, masking tape, sanding discs, disc adhesive, and an assortment of other things that the guys wanted, and he handed me a list.

I liked Emmitt and was eager to do whatever he asked.

About that time, Emmitt whistled at a fellow (Don White) who was walking over at the 'car line' pushing his own department's cart. The Passenger Car Assembly Line was located adjacent to the 'truck line'.

Don was headed upstairs to get supplies for the car version of our 'Paint Repair' department.

When Don walked over, Emmitt asked him... "Can you take Denny upstairs with you and teach him the ropes?", and Don smiled and nodded 'yes'.

I went over and grabbed our department's cart, and caught up to Don, and the two of us headed upstairs (to some far-off mysterious location?).

Right away I liked Don, he was heavy set like me, and a very soft-spoken gentleman, in his early thirties. He had long hair and a big moustache, coupled with a great big smile, and it was obvious that he was an insider who knew what was going on. So, I followed him.

As I have already mentioned... GM was a full mile long from the north end to the south end. Much of it was a single 20-30-foot level, but as you approached the southern end it became two stories at some point, with escalators and elevators, and stairways that provided access to the second level.

One of the elevators (one that we would be using on a regular basis to get our supplies) was large enough to lift as many as four vehicles at one time. With 20-30 foot ceilings on the second floor as well as the first, the place was simply 'cavernous' and it took this kind of oversized machinery to move things around in this huge plant.

As I would calculate later... Getting supplies was a good two-hour task, mostly because of the slow walk that wasn't required, but still implemented confidently by Don.

As Don and I walked there together for the first time (wherever it was that we were headed?) I got to know him, and ironically it turned out that I knew his wife!

She and I were previously acquainted because she was my post office lady of many years from the Irvington Annex. This seemed to cement us together as friends.

As we walked by all the different areas that were required to assemble trucks, Don stopped to explain what was taking place, and to 'meet & greet' people that he knew along the way. He kindly introduced me to everyone.

On this first trip, I must have telegraphed a sense of urgency to complete this task, and more than once Don politely told me to relax. He added that if Emmitt gave you this job, he trusts you. He also said that Emmitt knows what's going on, so don't worry.

―

Eventually I settled into Don's very slow, and methodical pace, and I did my best to enjoy the entire experience.

Why? Because I was lucky enough to be able to.

When we reached our destination, we came to an area about a hundred and fifty feet by maybe seventy-five feet. It was surrounded by a floor to ceiling cyclone fence, with a latched gate. Right in front of the gate was a large bench against a wall.

The gate had a small opening over a shallow shelf, which reminded me of the ticket booth in an old theatre. It was here that you conducted your business.

Don leaned on that shelf, and then turned towards me, and he said... "Take a seat on the bench. Watch and learn."

I could see three or four guys all the way against the far wall, who were playing cards. Don called one of the guys by name, and that guy set his cards down and came over. They exchanged pleasantries, and then Don asked to buy two burritos.

The Hispanic fellow reached down and extracted two foil wrapped burritos from a cooler and handed them to Don. Don gave the guy three bucks, and the guy took Don's list. He opened the gate and retrieved Don's cart. Don took a seat next to me on the bench out front and started eating one of his burritos. He held the other one up and wiggled it in the air, but said nothing, and kept eating.

About twenty minutes later the gatekeeper returned with Don's cart, and it was loaded with everything that was on Don's list. The guy opened the gate and rolled Don's cart out to where we were sitting on that bench. Then he immediately closed the gate; latching it and then he walked back to the table where he had been playing cards.

The gatekeeper never acknowledged my presence.

Then Don held up the uneaten burrito again and shook it a couple of more times. Then he turned away and left with his cart full of supplies, leaving me on that bench by myself.

I sat there waiting for the guy to finish up his card game, but it never happened... Finally, I stood up, and walked over to the gate and I yelled... "Excuse me?" ... nothing.

I waited a couple of minutes then tried getting that fellows attention again... "Excuse me?" ... Nothing!

Finally, it occurred to me that the solution to my problem was in that burrito that Don held up. The one that he was wiggling in the air... Suddenly, I had an epiphany.

"Excuse me, can I buy a couple of burritos?" I asked.

Immediately the guy stood up and came over. He pulled two burritos from that cooler, then he opened the gate, let me and my cart inside, and then he closed and latched the gate behind me.

Then he turned and walked back to his card game, and sat down... I pushed my cart a little further into the enclosed area, and waited again, but nothing happened.

Finally, the guy turned towards me, somewhat exasperated, and he pointed towards the rows of inventory... saying... "Go ahead, help yourself! Let me know when you have everything that you need"

I took the hint, finally... and I rummaged through the rows and rows of inventory selecting the items that were on the list, placing each item in the cart before moving on to the next row, to see if there was something there that was on my list.

Once I had retrieved everything, I came back to the area just inside the gate and the guy came over. I handed him my list, thinking that he'd want to double check what I took, but all he did was grab my list away from me, crumpled it up and tossed it into a garbage can. Then he smiled and said... "See you next week." And using his hand he directed me out of the area where he latched the gate behind me.

I have never been incarcerated but after this experience, I imagined that those around me probably had prison experience, and I surmised that this is probably what it must be like in prison? It's a system of who oversaw any given area.

Slowly I made my way back to 'Paint Repair'. The next week I repeated most of this experience with Don again. He laughed when I told him how I had finally learned the secret of getting supplies.

After my lessons were complete, I was the supply-guy for almost a year.

Intuitive Larry

As the weeks marched on, I learned to love those walks with Don, and I loved being in Larry Pimentel's good graces as we were becoming good friends as well.

One day as I arrived to start work, Larry yelled my name, and flagged me over. I walked over to his area to see what he wanted. He told me that it seemed like I was interested in the drivers over on the 'Short-Line' and I confirmed that I was. That's when he said... "OK. Then today I want you to go over and drive."

From that point forward, each day when I arrived, Larry would see me walking into the 'Paint Repair" area, and he'd motion and point with his arms, for me to drive. He used a kind of swooping motion with his arms and hands, almost like a maestro does when directing an orchestra.

I never worked in 'Paint Repair" again.

Picking Joe's Brain

I drove vehicles off that 'Short-Line' for about six months. One day as I was bringing a truck back onto the 'Short-Line' track for another pass, I stopped to talk with Joe. I had secretly named this guy the Casino Operator.

Joe was your stereo-typical pimp looking African American. He was ALWAYS impeccably dressed and had that traditional huge pimp hat on - every day.

Let me repeat that if you didn't get it? He wore a great big pimp hat EVERYDAY.

He was supposed to be the guy who moved the trucks from the stopping point (in front of the automated track) onto the track. At least that was his official job. He had a stool and a podium at the beginning of the tracks, but all I ever saw him do there, was read a newspaper, or a magazine.

When a brand-new driver brought a truck over for the first time and acted like he or she was just going to drop the truck off... Joe flagged them with his hand (behind his back no less) and he motioned to them, to drive the trucks onto the moving conveyor belt themselves.

Soon all the truck delivery people knew better than to just drop a truck off for Joe to move. They learned fast that it was up to them to get that truck onto the conveyor system. As Joe put it... "Sometimes I need to train these chumps."

And ironically, that's exactly what he ended up doing. Subsequently, Joe hardly ever lifted his head up from the newspaper, or magazine that he was reading.

One day when I was over at Joe's location I asked him... "Hey Joe, what's your secret?"

Immediately he sensed what kind of information I was digging for, and he gave me the once over from head to toe, and then he said... "The first thing you need to do is dress better! You look like you're waiting for someone to tell you what to do next. You need to be in command. Dress, and act, like you own the place, and no one will ever try to put you to work."

Then he turned away where he resumed reading his newspaper. Apparently, he was done conversing with me, and I walked away, carrying with me Joe's million-dollar advice.

The next day I came in looking like more like Dean Gillespie, than Denny Magic.

I looked like I was headed downtown, and certainly NOT to work at GM. Larry motioned for me to drive, and when I arrived at the 'Short-Line', the other drivers said... "Hey, look at you - dude!"

After about a week of 'dressing up' Joe happened to walk by me, on his way to the break area so he could conduct the gambling session for lunch, with his attaché case full of professional gambling chips.

He took one look at the way I was dressed, and he reached out to shake my hand and said... "Way to go brother! Looking good!" and then he continued, on his way.

Soon thereafter, I had occasion to meet up with Joe in his area again, so I asked him... "Joe, I want to ask you something?" He stopped reading and looked up at me, "Yeah?", he asked?

I said... "I can see that you oversee things here, but why do you even work at GM?"

Joe laughed, and replied... "Look, I come here to gamble, not to work. But you have to have one of these..." and he flicked his ID badge... "Or you can't even get in here. I make more money gambling then I ever could in simple wages."

At that point things became somewhat more clear to me. GM was offering me a plethora of lesson in life that I was previously unaware of.

Same Schedule, Different Job

Driving on the short line was a great position to have been lucky enough to acquire. However, being associated with the 'Short-Line' meant that I STILL had to keep the same work schedule as the guys working for 'Paint Repair'.

That meant, that I still had to work 14 hour days, and every other weekend... But although I am not a religious man, every morning when I got home, despite those killer hours - I still thanked God!

Larry is Obviously Angry

One day instead of pointing me towards the 'Short-Line' Larry flagged me over to talk with him... When I arrived at his area he said... "Come on, let's take a walk.".

So, I followed him to a quiet place on the car side of the spray booth.

He stopped and looked a bit angry, and then he said... "What the fuck are you doing with your checks, eating them?". Immediately I was perplexed and answered, "I'm not sure what you mean?"

He sighed and said... "Look, accounting is all over my ass, about this. So, I need to know, how many check do you have at home laying around, uncashed?"

Suddenly I realized what this was all about... "Oh that." I answered.

He added… "Please do me a favor and cash those sons-a-bitches, so I can get accounting off my ass, alright?". I nodded and followed him back to the 'Paint Repair' department, where he motioned for me to go over and drive at the 'Short-Line'. He seemed disgusted with me and walked back to the 'Paint Repair' area alone.

Up to that point I had never seen Larry so irritated, and I never wanted to see it again.

No Checks Please?

I am only adding this part of the story because it was so damned sad, that it was funny... One night that Czechoslovakian fellow (Ralphs practical joke victim - mentioned earlier) became a somewhat regular driver in the final area.

He had been coming down to drive every night after the main line shut down, and the area that they assigned him was where more detailed mechanical fixes were undertaken. And, for the most part he was just fine. However, I am not sure if he did not possess good English Reading Skills, or he was just careless?

In any event, he jumped into a truck over in his area, and tossed the sign that was hanging on the steering wheel, into the back seat.

He started up the truck and with complete confidence he backed out of the stall, slammed it into drive and took off with that vehicle out the door to park it in the 'to be shipped' area outside.

Unfortunately for him, that sign read… "NO BRAKES".

Yes, you guessed it, he had a heavy foot, and he was unable to stop, slamming into eight other brand-new trucks, for a total of nine wrecks.

No one was hurt. And the guy was not fired, but GM paid dearly for that little mistake.

Another little Pow-Wow with Larry

Then one day; as I arrived for work, Larry flagged me over to his area, and once again he said... "Take a walk with me, we need to talk about something." So, I followed, and we went back to that quiet spot next to the spray booth.

Frankly I suspected that my world was going to come crashing down around me. No one could have the kind of continuing good luck, like I was experiencing. Everything eventually ends. And I was getting ready for the axe to fall.

Then Larry starts... "Now listen and listen carefully, as you may know, this plant has a 130 Quality Program, which we have had trouble winning." I had heard about that... it was a rewards program for plants that had superb quality results, and when they could achieve that 130 status, General Motors gave out some token award to everyone who worked there as an acknowledgment of their employee's service dedication.

I also knew that the Fremont plant had not received that award in many years. In fact, quality, had slipped so badly at the Fremont location that there was talk of closing the entire plant down and letting all 3,000+ employees go... So far it was just a rumor, but it was a scary one that didn't get repeated too much, for fear that it might come true.

Then Larry seemed to get REAL SERIOUS. He paused and then he said... "Of all the guys on this team, you have the most insight, and I trust you. So, here's what I want to tell you, and for God's sake don't let a word of this get out to anyone, not even your family. I mean this is huge, and it can't leak out. In fact, if it does, I won't be able to help you! If you tell anyone, you'll be on your own, and it will certainly cost you your job."

All I could do was silently nod that I could be trusted. Then he reached out and grabbed my shoulder... "OK. Here it is. In a few minutes, I'm going to walk you over to another section of the plant to meet Budd Greer, who is a foreman over there. But more importantly, Budd will be running a clandestine program from within the plant. He can give you all the details himself but suffice it to say that you will be taking orders directly from Budd from this day forward. Denny, you're the most qualified paint expert that we have..." he paused to correct himself... , "Well you and one other guy that we selected... who will be working on the same crew. He'll be working on days too."

I asked, "So, I won't be working nights anymore?"

Larry shook his head 'no' and said... "No. You'll be working with a small hand selected group of real experts. Budd has taken over a small building at the northwest corner of the plant, and that's where you'll be reporting to every day."

I wanted to know a few more details, so I asked... "Sounds like this new job comes a whole lot of potential risks? Can you tell me what some of the benefits will be?"

Larry smiled (something he rarely did) and he gave my shoulder a slight squeeze. "Look, Budd will tell you about any opportunities that will come your way, himself." He paused and gave me a very intense look... "Are you in?"

I nodded that I was, and he said... "OK. Then let's walk over and I'll introduce you to Budd."

The two of us walked quite a distance over to the Northeast corner of the plant where Budd was working as a foreman at the end of the passenger car line.

Larry caught Budd's attention, and we walked over as Larry motioned towards a large open door that led to the outside, and the three of us stepped outside the plant, so we could talk where it was quiet

Larry introduced me to Budd, and Budd shook my hand. Then Budd said, "Welcome aboard the Swat Team."

Larry smiled for the second time in all the years that I knew him, and he said... "Take care kid, and good luck!" And he walked away.

Budd motioned for me to follow him, and he walked with me along a pathway to a small, secluded building at the northwest corner of the plant. Not only was the building secluded but it looked like no one had been in it for decades.

There was no doubt that any of the regular employees, let alone any big-shots from 'corporate' would ever venture out this far. When we arrived, Budd unlocked the door, and we entered.

Budd switched on a light, and then he turned to me and said... "Now I want you to take a few days off, to acclimate to this change to day shift. In fact, don't come in until next Monday, at 6 am. But come to this building, don't even go back to "Paint Repair' and if you see any of the guys from there, or anyone else that you may know... DO NOT tell them anything about what you're doing, don't mention the swat team or anything about this operation."

I agreed, and we exited the building leaving it as we had found it.

I spent the weekend catching up on some sleep and wondering what the hell I had gotten myself into. All I knew for sure was that I trusted Larry impeccably, and with the little bit of information that I was given so far, I was willing to roll the dice.

Breaking Ground

When Monday arrived, I was still a bit fatigued, but I managed to get some sleep during this time off, so I got up on time, made my way into the plant along with the day shift as if nothing was different.

I suspect that the powers behind the "Swat Team" must have decided to shift me over to days, so that there was less chance of me mingling with my old night-shift-coworkers, and therefore being hit with a barrage of questions.

I made my way through the employee traffic all the way to the northwest corner of the plant, and outside the main building over to the little secret location.

When I arrived, I was greeted by a wonderful guy named Tom Walker. Tom already knew everything about the game plan, and he knew that I'd have a million questions, and he was ready to answer them all.

Of course, the first thing was why the new organization was being called "The Swat Team" ... Tom laughed and said that it seemed appropriate, seeing as our job was to swat anything that was wrong with our trucks -away.

Then he went into detail. He said... "As you may already know, this plant has a poor reputation for quality, and almost always has. Because of that, the guys in Detroit want to close us down, and fire everyone in it. That would include all the big shots in the front office. They can kiss their annual bonuses good-bye. And... When you combine day and night shift together... that's more than 3,000 people who will also lose their jobs."

He continued... "So, Budd and us guys will create a team of specialized experts who are craftsmen in their respective fields. We have an expert mechanic an air-con man, a top-drawer electrician, a guy who is a body and adjustment guy, an upholstery and trim expert, and now we have you as our paint repair guy. Between our crew on days, and the matching crew on nights, we should be able to bring any truck that is earmarked for 'surgical level' inspection, up to a status of 100% perfection. The goal is to achieve a 130 status."

Tom paused, and then said... "If you somehow get caught out here or attached in any way to 'The Swat Team' you'll be fired immediately... and you'll have zero recourse. Even the UAW won't be able to help you." He paused...

Then he added, "That's the bad news... The good news is this."

And this is where the story gets interesting... Tom explained... " First Budd has been punching your timecard in and out every day that you've been off getting ready for this. So, yes... you'll be paid for the whole week."

Then he paused... "Your work day will drop from fourteen to eight hours, but Budd will continue to punch your timecard in and out, so you'll be paid as if you're still working the same 14 hour days like you were in 'Paint Repair'. In addition, no more weekends, but Budd will still punch your card in and out, so you'll still get paid as if you're still working weekends. By the way, your work week will also be cut to four days a week with every Friday off. And again, Budd will punch you in and out."

Then Tom smiled and added... "Fridays you'll be paid but you're not totally off the hook. Every Friday you'll be required to arrive at my house in Milpitas by five o'clock in the afternoon, where you'll participate with the rest of the crew in a FREE steak BBQ and Margaritas, followed by "Choir Practice" which is essentially a meeting that Budd wants to have with all of us to discuss what happened during the week."

Tom could gauge by my expression that I was onboard. That's when he started talking shop... "OK. Here's how things are going to go down. One of our guys has a key to the lock on that fence out there (he pointed) which leads to Pacific Motor Transit's parking lot. As a truck ships, it is inspected one last time, before being handed off to Pacific Motor Transport, who takes possession of it, and then they move it to their lot on the other side of that fence. At that point GM doesn't own it any more. Now. When the big shots from corporate in Detroit come out for a surprise inspection, they'll walk the PMT lot and they'll place a florescent orange sticker on the windshield of every truck that they want to 'critically inspect' with a fine-tooth comb. They do that one day with the intention of driving all those marked trucks back onto the GM property the next day, so they can bring them into a special inspection room that is covered floor to ceiling, with white tiles and outfitted with huge bright lights, that way they can see every detail clearly. You understand everything so far?" I nodded that I did.

Tom smiled and then continued... "Our goal is to get those trucks in this building so we can catch everything that is wrong and fix it. Once we do that, we'll sneak the truck back into the PMT lot, and let nature take over. If we do our job, the corporate inspection team from Detroit will issue this plant a score of 130, and we'll be able to help keep this plant open. We'll be saving more than 3,000 jobs."

Sarcastically I added... "And we'll be helping to ensure that the guys in the front office still get a Christmas bonus."

Tom laughed and said... "Yeah that's also true!"

Over the course of the following days, I had a chance to meet the other fellows on our team. They were a very interesting crew of motley characters.

Truthfully I don't recall anyone's name, and I would not reveal that even if I could. The fact is, those guys and me worked to ensure that every truck that we worked on from the PMT lot was re-inspected, and each time there was a surprise inspection, it was The Swat Team that made sure that the Fremont Plant received a 130 score for quality.

The first time it happened... The Fremont plant earned a special commemorative drinking mug, and the big shots in the front office distributed one to every employee on days, and every employee on nights.

Those mugs were printed with a label that touted the perfect score of 130 and bragged about the top quality that Fremont had achieved.

I worked with the Swat Team until the plant was finally closed three years later.

I brought a portable typewriter into that little "Swat Team" building, and that is where I essentially started my writing career.

Not one person who was not associated with The Swat Team suspected what was going on in that little building, or had any idea, how close they came to losing their jobs.

To me the whole experience was an adventure and reminded me of what it must be like working for the CIA. All I can say is... Wow!

Changes

A lot of things have changed in the past thirty or forty years. The Fremont General Motors Assembly Plant building... is still right where it stood all those years ago, only now it's owned by Elon Musk and they call it Tesla®

The country has gone through a couple of recessions, and the American Automobile Industry almost disappeared, and then in 2016, it experienced one of its best years ever. Sales of automobiles and trucks were at an all-time high.

The guys (and gal) that I worked with in 'Paint Repair' and the men that I worked with on the 'Swat Team' were a wonderful collection of unique individuals who I often think about. For those that are no longer with us, I thank you all for your dedication. For those that may still be alive and well... I wish all of you the best!

For the rest of you... Thank you for taking this adventure with me! I have wanted to write this story for decades because it needed to be told!

About the author

Denny Magic was born in 1949 in San Francisco, California. He's a retired Hardware/Software Test Engineer, and has worked for many of the big names in the Silicon Valley.

In the early 1980's Denny started writing Stage Plays, Teleplays, Screenplays, and is a published writer of freelance magazine articles. He has written several Children's Story Books (including two with children's author Jeanne Wood, and one with author Kyle Axile). In 2012 he partnered with author Robert Steacy, and together the two wrote what they consider the Final Episode [#6 in the series] of "The Pirates of the Caribbean" franchise.

While working in the engineering field he started his own entertainment production company with partners Randel Chow & Jerry Mahdik, and together they produced several commercial CD projects into the late 1990's, which included two Disney® style musicals, and original Opera, plus one contemporary [easy rock] CD.

In 2006 Denny formed "Denny Magic Studios" which was a California Design Company specializing in Rides, Attractions, and Concessions for Theme Parks, with an emphasis on the Disney® style of 'Dark Rides' (rides that are inside buildings, using animatronic characters, music, and strong storytelling).

The company utilized freelance animators & artists, a conservative number of Creative Writers, and over a dozen gifted music composers from various countries around the world.

more than 40 short stories published with Amazon.com as of 2021

www.dennymagicl.com

Audio Versions available from Audible.Com

51

Made in the USA
Columbia, SC
11 September 2024